*The Story of a Special Day*
*Volume 71*

# March 11

70th day of the year
(71st in leap years)
295 days remaining
until the end of the year.

by Michael Dobson

Timespinner
Press

For more information about the series, about me, or about your special day, please email us at editor@timespinnerpress.com.

Look for other volumes in *The Story of a Special Day,* coming often.

# Table of Contents

**Cover:** Statue of Pharaoh Tuthmosis III, who died March 11, 1479 BCE.

**Back Cover:** The month of March, from the French Gothic illuminated manuscript *Les Très Riches Heures du duc de Berry*

# March 11 Quotations

"I came out of Bataan and I shall return!"

> — *General Douglas MacArthur, who left the Philippines on March 11, 1942*

"A learning experience is one of those things that say, 'You know that thing you just did? Don't do that.'"

> — *Douglas Adams, born March 11, 1952*

"If you're going to be a good and faithful judge, you have to resign yourself to the fact that you're not always going to like the conclusions you reach. If you like them all the time, you're probably doing something wrong."

> — *Justice Antonin Scalia, born March 11, 1936*

"The world has arrived at an age of cheap complex devices of great reliability; and something is bound to come of it."

> — *Vannevar Bush, born March 11, 1890*

"Few men during their lifetime come anywhere near exhausting the resources dwelling within them. There are deep wells of strength that are never used."

> — *Admiral Richard E. Byrd, died March 11, 1957*

# Johnny Appleseed Day

Although Johnny Appleseed is often considered an American tall tale in the tradition of Paul Bunyan and John Henry, the character is quite real. Jonathan Chapman, born September 26, 1774, got his start tending orchards as an apprentice in Massachusetts and Pennsylvania. Adopting a nomadic lifestyle, he moved into the frontier lands of Ohio, Indiana, Illinois, and present-day West Virginia, introducing apple trees wherever he went.

Rather than sow apple seeds at random, Johnny Appleseed planted nurseries, built fences around them, and arranged for the young trees to be sold on shares. Every year or so he would return to tend each nursery. Johnny Appleseed-planted nurseries are known to exist in northwest Pennsylvania and in the Mohican area of north-central Ohio.

The apples he planted weren't primarily for eating, but rather for producing hard cider and apple jack. In addition, in some areas settlers were required to plant orchards of apples and pears in order to claim land.

Johnny Appleseed was also a missionary for the Swedenborgian faith. He preached the Gospel to Native Americans, converting many. He lived a subsistence lifestyle, going barefoot and wearing old clothes. Whether he really wore the tin-pot hat for which he is famous is uncertain. In addition to his famous apple-planting, Johnny Appleseed was also sensitive to all animals, including insects, becoming a vegetarian in later life.

Different reports exist concerning his death, and even the site of his grave is a matter of controversy. Two competing sites in Fort Wayne, Indiana claim to be his final resting place. He lived until at least the age of 80 in spite of (or perhaps because of) the extreme privation of his life. He left a substantial estate of over 1,200 acres of valuable nurseries to his sister.

Johnny Appleseed Day is celebrated either on March 11 or September 26. September 26 is his birthday, but March 11 is often preferred because it is during planting season. There is also an annual Johnny Appleseed Festival in Lisbon, Ohio, on September 18-19. Numerous books and films honor both his legend and his reality.

JOHNNY APPLESEED.

# March 11 Holidays and Celebrations

## Independence Day (Lithuania)

Lithuania actually celebrates two Independence Days, the first on February 16 to celebrate its independence from the Russian and German Empires in 1918, and on March 11 to celebrate its re-establishment and independence from the Soviet Union in 1990.

## Moshoeshoe Day (Lesotho)

King Moshoeshoe I (1786 — March 11, 1870) was ruler and military leader of what was then known as Basutoland. He fought numerous wars with Zulu, Boer, and British invaders, losing some ground but never suffering a major defeat. He established the modern-day boundaries of Lesotho. His death marked the end of the traditional period and the beginning of the colonial era. When Lesotho regained independence, it reestablished itself as a constitutional monarchy. Moshoeshoe Day is held every year on March 11 to commemorate the day of his death.

King Moshoeshoe I (seated with top hat)

## Christian Feast Days

Saints commemorated on March 11 include Aengus the Culdee, Alberta of Agen, Aurea of San Millán, Constantine, Blessed John Righi, Sophronius of Jerusalem, and Vindician.

# What Happened on March 11?

## 1784 CE - Treaty of Mangalore

The Second Anglo-Mysore War took place in Mughal India between the Kingdom of Mysore and the British East India Company. Mysore was a key French ally in India. When the French entered the American Revolutionary War on the side of the colonists, British forces seized a French port in Mysore, sparking the war. After the worst defeat of the British East India Company to date, the British accepted a humiliating peace in the Treaty of Mangalore, signed on March 11, 1784.

## 1824 CE - Bureau of Indian Affairs Founded

The Bureau of Indian Affairs, today part of the U.S. Department of the Interior, administers and manages over 55 million acres of land held in trust for Native Americans. The bureau was established on March 11, 1824, originally as part of the Department of War.

## 1848 CE - First Democratically Elected Canadian Prime Ministers

On March 11, 1848, the first democratically elected Canadian prime ministers, Louis-Hippolyte Lafontaine and Robert Baldwin, took office. At the time, the United Province of Canada was divided into Canada East and Canada West, and so the office of prime minister was shared between the two.

## 1851 CE - **First Performance of** *Rigoletto*

The first performance of Giuseppe Verdi's opera *Rigoletto* took place on March 11, 1851, at La Fenice in the city of Venice. While it had initial troubles with Austrian censors, it became recognized as one of the masterpieces of Verdi's career. Another of Verdi's operas, *Don Carlos*, premiered on March 11, 1867, this time in Paris.

## 1861 CE - **The Confederacy Adopts a Constitution**

On March 11, 1861, the Confederate States of America adopted its constitution, which was mostly a word-for-word duplicate of the United States Constitution — except, of course, for sections on states' rights and slavery.

## 1864 CE - **The Great Sheffield Flood**

The largest man-made disaster ever to befall England took place on March 11, 1864, when the Dale Dyke Dam broke, releasing more than 700 million gallons of water. The resultant flood killed 238 people, drowned 700 animals, destroyed 130 buildings, and swept away 15 bridges, devastating the town of Sheffield.

# 1888 CE - The Great Blizzard of 1888

In one of the most severe recorded blizzards in American history, snowfalls of up to 50 inches fell in parts of New Jersey, New York, Massachusetts, and Connecticut from March 111 to March 14, 1888. It produced snowdrifts over 50 feet high, paralyzing the East Coast from the Chesapeake region to the Canadian Maritimes. More than 400 died.

The Brooklyn Bridge during the Great Blizzard of 1888

# 1941 CE - FDR Signs the Lend-Lease Act

Effectively ending the pretence of American neutrality in World War II, the Lend-Lease Act established a program by which the US would supply the UK, the Soviet Union, China, Free France, and other Allied nations to resist the Axis powers. Over $50 billion in Lend-Lease was shipped, the equivalent of $650 billion today.

President Franklin D. Roosevelt signs the Lend-Lease Act into law

# 1942 CE - Douglas MacArthur Leaves Corregidor

As Japanese forces continued to tighten their grip on the Philippines, President Franklin D. Roosevelt ordered General Douglas MacArthur to leave the island fortress of Corregidor to take up command in Australia. Though MacArthur protested, he complied, leaving the rocky island with a small party on the night of March 11, 1942, in a flotilla of four PT boats.

# 1945 CE - Operation Tan No. 2 (第二次丹作戰)

In the Pacific theater of World War II, Operation Tan No. 2 was a long range kamikaze mission aimed at the Allied fleet anchorage at Ulithi Atoll. Twenty-four twin-engine bombers took off on March 11, 1945. Mechanical difficulties and fuel problems meant that only two of the aircraft reached Ulithi. One hit the carrier USS *Randolph*, killing 27 and wounding 105. The second thought an access road and signal tower on a nearby island was a ship and crashed into the road, killing no one but the aircraft crew.

USS *Randolph* after the attack, showing the damage

# 1977 CE - Hanafi Siege Ends

From March 9-11, 1977, twelve African-American Muslim gunmen led by Hamaas Abdul Khaalis took 149 hostages, killing two and wounding one, and captured three buildings in Washigton, DC. After a 39-hour standoff, a combination of US law enforcement and the intervention of Muslim ambassadors from Egypt, Pakistan, and Iran, the remaining hostages were freed. All the attackers were tried and convicted; the leader receiving a sentence of 21 to 120 years in prison.

# 1978 CE - Coastal Road Massacre

In the Coastal Road Massacre, Fatah militants led by Abu Jihad hijacked an Israeli bus, killing 38 civilians, including 13 children, and wounding 71. The original target was a luxury hotel in Tel Aviv, but through a navigation error, the attackers ended up 40 miles north of their target. It was at the time the worst terrorist attack in Israel's history. Israel responded with Operation Litani, also known as the 1978 South Lebanon Conflict.

## 2004 CE - Madrid Train Bombings

On March 11, 2004, a date known as 11-M in Spain, terrorists set off a series of ten explosions on the Madrid commuter train system, killing 191 and wounding 1,800. Some of the details, including exactly who was behind the bombings, are still the subject of controversy.

## 2011 CE - Tōhoku Earthquake and Tsunami

On March 11, 2011, a magnitude 9.03 undersea earthquake off the Pacific coast of Tōhoku, a region of Japan. It was one of the five most powerful recorded earthquakes in history. The tsunami waves that resulted reached heights of up to 133 feet, killing or injuring over 24,000 people and destroying or damaging nearly a million buildings. The tsunami also resulted in serious damage to the Fukushima Daiichi Nuclear Power Plant complex. Total economic damage was estimated at $235 billion, making it the most expensive natural disaster in world history.

Part of the damage at the Fukushima Nuclear Reactor

# Who Was Born on March 11?

*The abbreviation "O.S." on some dates refers to the fact that the Russian Empire did not switch from the Julian to the Gregorian calendar at the same time as the rest of Europe, and therefore some figures have two dates for their birth or death.*

*People whose original names are not in the Western alphabet have their native names in the appropriate script shown in parenthesis.*

## Acting and Modeling

### Rob Brown (March 11, 1984 — )

Rob Brown starred in the HBO series *Treme.*

### Melissa Rycroft (March 11, 1983 — )

Former Dallas Cowboys cheerleader and reality star Melissa Rycroft has been a contestant on *The Bachelor,* appeared in the reality TV series *Dallas Cowboys Cheerleaders: Making the Team,* and on two seasons of *Dancing With The Stars.* She was named one of *People* Magazine's Most Beautiful People in 2009 and to *Maxim* Magazine's "Hot 100."

## Lindsey McKeon (March 11, 1982 — )

Actress Lindsey McKeon appeared on *Guiding Light, One Tree Hill*, and *Saved by the Bell: The New Class*.

## Thora Birch (March 11, 1982 — )

Thora Birch was in the Academy Award-winning *American Beauty* and received a Golden Globe nomination for her role in *Ghost World*.

## Heidi Cortez (March 11, 1981 — )

Heidi Cortez was the radio host of Howard Stern's Sirius XM satellite channel, published the best-selling *Heidi's Bedtime Stories,* and appeared on the reality show *Sunset Tan*.

## David Anders (March 11, 1981 — )

David Anders played Julian Stark on *Alias* and Adam Monroe on *Heroes*.

## Eric the Midget (March 11, 1975 — )

Eric Lynch became known as Eric the Midget as a member of *The Howard Stern Show's* Wack Pack, though he prefers Eric the Actor. He suffers from numerous health issues, but claims to have outlived every doctor's prediction for his life expectancy.

# Johnny Knoxville (March 11, 1971 — )

Johnny Knoxville (real name Philip John Clapp) is best known as co-creator of the MTV series *Jackass*.

Johnny Knoxville

## Terrence Howard (March 11, 1969 — )

Terrence Howard's first major role was in 1995's *Mr. Holland's Opus*, but he is perhaps best known as Rhodey in the *Iron Man* films.

## Wallace Langham (March 11, 1965 — )

Actor Wallace Langham played David Hodges in the TV series *CSI: Crime Scene Investigation.*

## Shane Ritchie (March 11, 1964 — )

Shane Ritchie played Alfie Moon in the long-running BBC soap opera *EastEnders.*

## Emma Chambers (March 11, 1964 — )

Emma Chambers has appeared in the BBC comedy *The Vicar of Dibley* and in the 1999 film *Notting Hill.*

## Alex Kingston (March 11, 1963 — )

Alex Kingston played Dr. Elizabeth Corday on the NBC drama *ER* and River Song in *Doctor Who*.

## Jeffry Nordling (March 11, 1962 — )

Jeffry Nordling played Larry Moss in *24* and Nick Bolen in *Desperate Housewives.*

## Elias Koteas (March 11, 1961 — )

Elias Koteas was in T*he Prophecy, Fallen,* and two *Teenage Mutant Ninja Turtles* films.

## Nina Hartley (March 11, 1959 — )

Award-winning pornographic actor Nina Hartley holds a *magna cum laude* nursing degree and works as a sex educator with a line of instructional videos and a book.

## Anissa Jones (March 11, 1958 — August 28, 1976)

Anissa Jones played Buffy on the CBS sitcom *Family Affair.* She died at the age of 18 from combined drug intoxication.

## The Lady Chablis (March 11, 1957 — )

Drag queen Lady Chablis (Benjamin Edward Knox) was featured in the book *Midnight in the Garden of Good and Evil* and played "herself" in the 1997 movie of the same name.

## Rob Paulsen (March 11, 1956 — )

Rob Paulsen won a Daytime Emmy as the voice of the cartoon character Pinky from *Pinky and the Brain.* He has been the voice of over 250 different animated characters.

Anissa Jones (top) and Johnny Whitaker,
publicity photo from *Family Affair*, 1967

## Susan Richardson (March 11, 1952 — )

Susan Richardson played Susan Bradford on the long-running TV series *Eight is Enough*.

## Dominique Sanda (March 11, 1951 — )

French actress Dominique Sanda appeared in numerous important European films of the 1970s, including *The Garden of the Finzi-Continis*, which won an Academy Award for Best Foreign Language Film.

## Mart Metcalf (March 11, 1946 — )

Mart Metcalf is best known for playing Doug Neidermeyer in 1978's *National Lampoon's Animal House*.

## Sandra Milo (March 11, 1935 — )

Sandra Milo is best known for her award-winning roles in Federico Fellini's films *8-1/2* and *Juliet of the Spirits*.

## Albert Salmi (March 11, 1957 — )

Actor Albert Salmi's first major role was in the 1958 film *The Brothers Karamazov*. He went on to play roles on *The Twilight Zone, Star Trek, Gunsmoke*, and many other television shows.

## Dorothy Gish (March 11, 1898 — June 4, 1968)

Actress Dorothy Gish, the younger sister of Lillian Gish, starred in numerous silent films.

Lillian and Dorothy Gish, *Orphans of the Storm,* 1921

**Shemp Howard** (March 11, 1895 —
November 22, 1955)

Shemp Howard, older brother of Moe and Curly
Howard, was the "third Stooge" in the early
years of The Three Stooges, returning to the role
in 1946 after Curly Howard suffered a stroke.

# Crime

### Joey Buttafuoco (March 11, 1956 — )

Auto body shop owner Joey Buttafuoco is best
known for his affair with Amy Fisher, who later
show Joey's wife Mary Jo Buttafuoco in the face.

# Fashion

### Jenny Packham (March 11, 1965 — )

British fashion designer Jenny Packman was
named Hollywood Style Designer of the Year
and International Couture Bridal Designer of the
Year in 2007, and Best British Bridal Designer
three times beginning in 2008.

# Film Production

## David Guggenheim (March 11, 1963 — )

David Guggenheim is the only filmmaker to have released three documentaries ranked in the top 100 highest-grossing documentaries of all time: *An Inconvenient Truth, It Might Get Loud,* and *Waiting for "Superman."*

## Peter Berg (March 11, 1962 — )

Peter Berg directed the film *Friday Night Lights* and developed the television series adapted from it. He also played Dr. Billy Kronk on the CBS drama *Chicago Hope.*

## Jerry Zucker (March 11, 1950 — )

Jerry Zucker directed the comedies *Airplane!, Naked Gun, Top Secret!,* and the romantic thriller *Ghost.*

## Martin Richards (March 11, 1932 — November 26, 2012)

Martin Richards won the Best Picture Academy Award for his production of *Chicago.*

**Raoul Walsh** (March 11, 1887 — December 31, 1980)

Raoul Walsh is known as the director of *The Big Trail, High Sierra*, and *White Heat,* with such stars as John Wayne, Humphrey Bogart, and James Cagney.

**David Horsley** (March 11, 1873 — February 23, 1933

David Horsley built the first film studio in Hollywood.

# Journalism and Letters

**Kieran Scott ("Kate Brian")** (March 11, 1974 — )

Best known for her young-adult novels written as "Kate Brian," including the *Private series,* Kieran Scott has also published a number of books under her own name, most famously *I Was a Non-Blonde Cheerleader.*

**Libba Bray** (March 11, 1964 — )

Young adult author Libba Bray wrote the New York *Times* bestseller *A Great and Terrible Beauty*, along with many other books.

## Fred M'membe (March 11, 1959 — )

Zambian journalist and editor of the *Zambia Post* Fred M'membe was named one of the World Press Freedom Heroes by the International Press Institute.

## Flemming Rose (March 11, 1958 — )

Dutch journalist and editor Flemming Rose published the cartoons that initiated the *Jyllands-Posten* Muhammad cartoons controversy.

## James Pinkerton (March 11, 1958 — )

Columnist and author James Pinkerton served on the White House staffs of Ronald Reagan and George H. W. Bush and serves as contributing editor and panelist for numerous print and online publications.

## D. J. MacHale (March 11, 1955 — )

Writer and director D. J. MacHale is the author of the popular young adult book series *Pendragon* and *Morpheus Road*. He has also worked on TV shows including *Are You Afraid of the Dark?*

## Douglas Adams (March 11, 1952 — May 11, 2001)

Douglas Adams is best known as the author of *The Hitchhiker's Guide to the Galaxy.*

"Don't Panic" symbol from *The Hitchhiker's Guide to the Galaxy*

## Sam Donaldson (March 11, 1934 — )

Long-time ABC journalist Sam Donaldson was the network's White House correspondent at different times from 1977 to 1999.

## Rupert Murdoch (March 11, 1931 — )

Media mogul Rupert Murdoch owns News Corporation, a conglomerate that owns Fox News, Twentieth Century Fox studios, Harper Collins publishers, *The Wall Street Journal*, and numerous other media properties.

## Ezra Jack Keats (March 11, 1916 — May 6, 1983)

Children's author and illustrator Ezra Jack Keats won the Caldecott Medal for *The Snowy Day,* and is credited with introducing multiculturalism into mainstream American children's literature.

## Ronald Syme (March 11, 1903 — September 4, 1989)

New Zealand-born historian Ronald Symes is generally regarded as one of the greatest historians of ancient Rome, and is best known for his 1939 book *The Roman Revolution*, covering Roman political life following the assassination of Julius Caesar.

# Military

## Sir Fitzroy MacLean (March 11, 1911 — June 15, 1996)

Scottish soldier and adventurer Fitzroy MacLean enlisted in the British Army as a private and rose to the rank of Brigadier. He wrote several books recounting his adventures in Soviet Central Asia and in commando raids behind enemy lines. Some suggest that MacLean was one of Ian Fleming's inspirations for James Bond.

# Music

## Lisa Loeb (March 11, 1968 — )

Singer-songwriter and actress Lisa Loeb was the first artist to have a number one single in the United States while not signed to a recording contract with 1994's "Stay (I Missed You)."

## Cheryl Lynn (March 11, 1957 — )

R&B and disco artist Cheryl Lynn is best known for her 1978 song "Got to Be Real," which reached #1 on the US R&B charts.

## Jimmy Fortune (March 11, 1955 — )

Jimmy Fortune sang tenor for the Statler Brothers for over two decades and wrote several number one hits for the group.

## David Newman (March 11, 1954 — )

Composer David Newman has scored nearly 100 feature films, including T*he War of the Roses, Hoffa, The Mighty Ducks, Bowfinger, The Freshman*, and many others.

## Bobby McFerrin (March 11, 1950 — )

Ten-time Grammy winner Bobby McFerrin is best known for his 1988 hit "Don't Worry, Be Happy."

## Lawrence Welk (March 11, 1903 — May 17, 1992)

"Champagne music" impressario Lawrence Welk hosted the long-running *The Lawrence Welk Show* from 1955 to 1982, and is ranked #43 on *TV Guide's* 50 Greatest TV Stars of All Time.

Lawrence Welk (right) with Norma Zimmer

# Poker

## Joel Hachem (جوزف هاشم) (March 11, 1968 — )

Lebanese-born Australian professional poker player Joel Hachem won his first title at the 2005 World Series of Poker, netting $7.5 million.

# Politics and Law

## Jesse Jackson, Jr. (March 11, 1965 — )

Son of civil rights leader Jesse Jackson, Jesse Jackson Jr. represented Illinois' 2nd Congressional District in Congress. He resigned from Congress in 2012 for mental and physical health problems, and was investigated by the House Ethics Committee and the FBI for financial improprieties.

## Antonin Scalia (March 11, 1936 — )

Antonin Scalia was appointed an Associate Justice of the Supreme Court in 1986 by Ronald Reagan.

## Robert Mosbacher (March 11, 1927 — January 27, 2010)

Robert Mosbacher was U.S. Secretary of Commerce from 1989 to 1992, founded the natural gas company Mosbacher Energy, and won numerous awards in competitive sailing.

## Ralph Abernathy (March 11, 1926 — April 17, 1990)

Civil rights leader Ralph Abernathy, a close associate of Martin Luther King Jr., took up the leadership of King's Southern Christian Leadership Conference, led the SCLC Poor People's Campaign, and also led the 1968 March on Washington.

## Harold Wilson (March 11, 1916 — May 24, 1995)

Harold Wilson was prime minister of the United Kingdom from 1964 to 1970, and from 1974 to 1976, winning four general elections.

# Science and Computers

## Nicolaas Bloembergen (March 11, 1920 — )

Physicist Nicolaas Bloembergen won the Nobel Prize in Physics for his work in laser spectroscopy, and also won the Lorentz Medal and the IEEE Medal of Honor.

## J. C. R. Licklider (March 11, 1915 — June 26, 1990)

Computer scientist J. C. R. Licklider, called "computing's Johnny Appleseed," was one of the first to foresee interactive computing. As an Internet pioneer, he helped inspire the graphical user interface and the ARPANET.

## Robert Havemann (March 11, 1910 — April 9, 1982)

Chemist and East German dissident Robert Havemann was arrested by the Gestapo for his involvement with the Communist Party, but his execution was postponed numerous times because he was needed to explain his research findings. After the war, the Americans barred him from research in West Berlin, so he became a professor in East Berlin. Subsequently, he came out against communist ideology and was put under house arrest until his death. He was awarded the title "Righteous Among the Nations" by the Israeli Holocaust Memorial, Yad Vashem.

## Vannevar Bush (March 11, 1890 — June 28, 1974)

Engineer and inventor Vannevar Bush was one of the administrators of the Manhattan Project, founded Raytheon, and served as chairman of NACA (predecessor of NASA) and as dean of the MIT School of Engineering. He received the Edison Medal, the National Medal of Science, and the Atomic Pioneer Award.

# Sports

## Anthony Davis (March 11, 1993 — )

NBA power forward and center Anthony Davis was the first overall selection in the 2012 NBA Draft, was named an NCAA Unanimous First Team All-American in 2012, and was named 2012 Player of the Year, among many other honors.

## Dan Uggla (March 11, 1980 — )

Second baseman Dan Uggla won the National League Silver Slugger Award in 2010 and was named *Sporting News* Rookie of the Year in 2006.

## Elton Brand (March 11, 1979 — )

Power forward and center Elton Brand was the NBA's co-Rookie of the Year in 2000, an All-Star in 2002 and 2006, and won three gold medals competing for the United States in the FIBA World and American Championships and the Goodwill Games.

## Becky Hammon (March 11, 1977 — )

WNBA basketball guard Becky Hammon was born and grew up in the United States and became a naturalized Russian citizen in 2008. She plays for the San Antonio Silver Stars and won a bronze medal at the 2008 Beijing Olympics as part of the Russian national team.

## Shawn Springs (March 11, 1975 — )

NFL cornerback Shawn Springs earned all-American honors in college football and was third overall in the 1997 NFL draft. He was named Big Ten Defensive Player of the Year in 1996.

## Bobby Abreu (March 11, 1974 — )

Born in Venzuela, Bobby Abreu is a baseball outfielder who has been a two-time All-Star, and won both a Gold Glove Award and a Silver Slugger Award. His nicknames include "El Comedulce" and "La Luche."

Bobby Abreu

## Eddie Lawson (March 11, 1958 — )

Motorcycle racer "Steady Eddie" Lawson won the Grand Prix motorcycle racing world championsip four times.

## César Gerónimo (March 11, 1948 — )

Dominican baseball player César Gerónimo was part of the Cincinnati Reds' "Big Red Machine" in the 1970s, winning four Gold Glove Awards.

## Dock Ellis (March 11, 1945 — December 19, 2008)

Pitcher Dock Ellis was named American League Comeback Player of the Year for helping to lead the New York Yankees to the 1976 World Series.

## Louise Brough (March 11, 1923 — )

Louise Brough is a former world #1 ranked female tennis player, winning four Wimbleton and one US championship tournaments.

# Who Died on March 11?

## Acting and Film

**Betty Hutton** (February 26, 1921 — March 11, 2007)

Betty Hutton made 19 films, including 1947's *The Perils of Pauline* and the 1950 musical *Let's Dance* with Fred Astaire, but is best known for her leading role as Annie Oakley in *Annie Get Your Gun*.

**Vince Edwards** (July 9, 1928 — March 11, 1996)

Vince Edwards is best known for playing TV doctor *Ben Casey* on the eponymous show.

**Richard Brooks** (May 8, 1912 — March 11, 1992)

Richard Brooks directed the 1955 film *Blackboard Jungle*, 1958's *Cat on a Hot Tin Roof*, and 1960's *Elmer Gantry*, winning an Academy Award for writing the latter screenplay.

## F. W. Murnau (December 28, 1888 — March 11, 1931)

Silent film director F. W. Murnau is best known for his 1922 film *Nosferatu*.

# Art and Architecture

## Benjamin West (October 10, 1738 — March 11, 1820)

American painter Benjamin West is best known for his historical scenes. His most famous painting, *The Death of General Wolfe,* was exhibited at the Royal Academy.

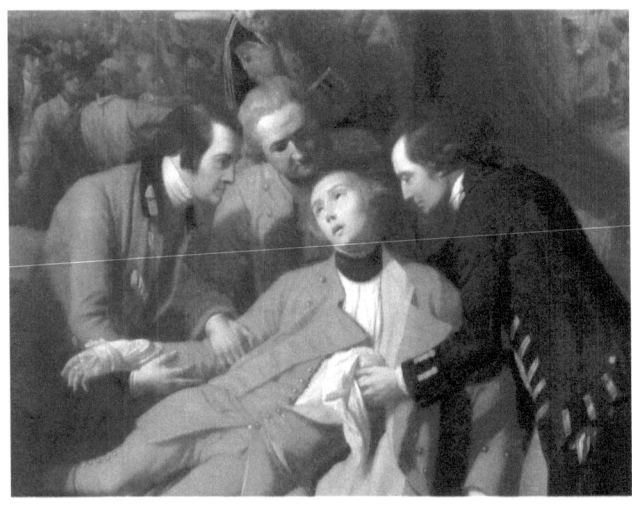

*The Death of General Wolfe* by Benjamin West

### Donato Bramante (1444 — March 11, 1514)

Donato Bramante developed the plan for St. Peter's Basilica in Rome, later executed by Michelangelo.

# Business

### Oscar Mayer (March 29, 1859 — March 11, 1955)

German-American butcher and sausage maker Oscar Mayer founded the processed meat firm of the same name.

The Oscar Mayer Wienermobile in the Henry Ford Museumt

## Joseph S. Cullinan (December 31, 1860 — March 11, 1937)

Oilman Joseph Cullinan founded The Texas Company, later known as Texaco.

# Exploration

### Roy Chapman Andrews (January 26, 1884 — March 11, 1960)

Explorer and adventurer Roy Chapman Andrews was director of the American Museum of Natural History. He led expeditions into the Gobi Desert and Mongolia, and brought the first known fossil dinosaur eggs to the museum.

### Richard E. Byrd (October 25, 1888 — March 11, 1957)

Admiral Richard E. Byrd is best known for his claims to have been the first to reach the North Pole and the South Pole by air. (The North Pole claim is disputed.) In addition, he was a pioneering aviator, crossing the Atlantic and Arctic Oceans. He received the Medal of Honor for his achievements.

President Calvin Coolidge awards the Medal of Honor to Richard Byrd (left, wearing the Medal and carrying a sword) and his pilot Floyd Bennett (right, receiving the Medal)

# Letters

### Erle Stanley Gardner (July 17, 1889 — March 11, 1970)

Prolific author Erle Stanley Gardner wrote nearly 150 novels, most famously the Perry Mason mystery series.

### John Wyndham (July 10, 1903 — March 11, 1969)

Science fiction writer John Wyndham is best known for his novels *The Day of the Triffids* and *The Midwich Cuckoos*, both of which were adapted into films, the latter renamed *Village of the Damned*.

### Hendrik Willem van Loon (January 14, 1882 — March 11, 1944)

Historian Hendrik Willem van Loon is best known for his history of the world written for children, *The Story of Mankind*, which won the first Newberry Medal in 1922.

### John Toland (November 30, 1670 — March 11, 1722)

Philosopher John Toland is best known for his 1696 book *Christianity not Mysterious*, which resulted in members of the Irish parliament proposing he be burned at the stake.

# Military

### William Rosencrans (September 6, 1819 — March 11, 1898)

Union Civil War general William Rosencrans won the battles of Iuka and Corinth in 1862 and outmaneuvered Confederate general Braxton Bragg in the Tullahoma Campaign, but came to disaster at the Battle of Chickamauga, where his losses led to him being relieved of command.

**John Forbes** (September 5, 1707 — March 11, 1759)

British general John Forbes captured the French outpost at Fort Duquesne during the French and Indian War, and is credited for naming the city of Pittsburgh, Pennsylvania.

# Music

**Geraldine Farrar** (February 28, 1882 — March 11, 1967)

American opera star and film actress Geraldine Farrar had a large fan base of young women known as Gerry-flappers. She starred in several silent films and received two stars on the Hollywood Walk of Fame, one for music and one for film.

Geraldine Farrar

# Politics and Public Affairs

## Slobodan Milošević (Слободан Милошевић) (August 20, 1941 — March 11, 2006)

Former President of Serbia and President of the Federal Republic of Yugoslavia, Milošević was charged with war crimes in connection with the wars in Bosnia, Croatia, and Kosovo in the 1990s.

## James Tobin (March 5, 1918 — March 11, 2002)

James Tobin served on the Council of Economic Advisors and the Board of Governors of the Federal Reserve System, and also taught at Harvard and Yale. He received the Nobel Prize in Economics in 1971. The idea of the "Tobin tax" on foreign exchange transactions to reduce speculation is one of his innovations.

## Whitney Young (July 31, 1921 — March 11, 1971)

Civil rights leader Whitney Young served as executive director of the National Urban League and received the Presidential Medal of Freedom in 1969.

(from left to right) Dr. Martin Luther King Jr., President Lyndon Johnson, Whitney Young, and James Farmer at the White House, January 1964

## Benjamin Waugh (February 20, 1839 — March 11, 1908)

Victorian social reformer Benjamin Waugh founded England's National Society for the Prevention of Cruelty to Children.

## Charles Sumner (January 6, 1811 — March 11, 1874)

Massachusetts senator Charles Sumner was the leader of the antislavery movement in Massachusetts and the chief Radical Republican leader in the Senate seeking to destroy slavery.

### Elagabalus (203 — March 11, 222)

Emperor of Rome from 218 to 222, Elagabalus was assassinated along with his mother by the Praetorian Guard. He is also considered to have invented the whoopie cushion.

*Cover Story*

### Thutmose III (1481 BCE — March 11, 1425 BCE)

Pharaoh Thutmose III served as co-regent with his stepmother Hatshepsut for 22 years before becoming sole pharaoh. His conquests created the largest empire in Egyptian history, from north Syria to Nubia. Thutmose III constructed over 50 temples and made major contributions to the Karnak complex.

# Science and Invention

### Philo Farnsworth (August 19, 1906 — March 11, 1971)

Inventor Philo Farnsworth made major contributions to the development of television, including the video camera tube. He was the first to demonstrate a working all-electronic television system to the public.

## Sir Alexander Fleming (August 6, 1881 — March 11, 1955)

Scottish biologist Sir Alexander F;eming won the Nobel Prize in Medicine for his discovery of penicillin.

# Sports

## Merlin Olsen (September 15, 1940 — March 11, 2010)

Merlin Olsen spent his 15-year NFL career with the Los Angeles Rams. He was elected to the Pro Football Hall of Fame and the College Football Hall of Fame. As an actor, he had a major role in the TV show *Little House on the Prairie* and starred in the NBC series *Father Murphy*.

## Bernie "Boom Boom" Geoffrion (February 14, 1931 — March 11, 2006)

Ice hockey player Bernie Geoffrion is credited as one of the inventors of the slapshot. He was inducted into the Hockey Hall of Fame in 1972.

The month of March, from the illuminated manuscript *Les Très Riches Heures du duc de Berry*

# March: The Third Month

In ancient Rome, March was the first month of the year. As the first month of spring, in the Mediterranean climate it marked the beginning of the military campaign season. That's why March (Martius) is named in honor of Mars, the Roman god of war.

Although the first month of the year was moved back to January sometime during the transition of Rome from a kingdom to a republic (historians differ), March was the first month of the year in Russia until the end of the 15th Century, and is the first month of the year in many other cultures and religions.

In the northern hemisphere, March 1 marks the beginning of meteorological spring. In the southern hemisphere, March is the equivalent of September, making southern hemisphere March the beginning of autumn.

March is one of the seven months that have 31 days in it. March starts on the same day of the week as November every year, and except for leap years starts on the same day as February. March starts on the same day of the week as the previous June except for leap years, and in leap years starts on the same day as the previous September and December.

## March in Other Cultures

In Finland, March is called *maaliskuu* (earthy month). In Ukraine, it's *березень* (birch tree). Other names for March include *Lentmona*t (Saxon), *Hyld-monath* (Angles), and *sušec* (Slovene).

## March Symbols

**B i r t h s t o n e s :** A q u a m a r i n e a n d b l o o d s t o n e , b o t h representing courage.

Aquamarine

# Birth Flowers: Daffodils

Daffodils in Bagatelle Park, Paris, France

# March Events

**Honorary months:** Presidents, Congresses, and nations around the world issue proclamations recognizing particular months to honor certain causes. These events generally fall in March. (All US unless otherwise noted.)

- National Nutrition Month

- American Red Cross Month

- Women's History Month (celebrated in Canada during October)

- Irish-American Heritage Month

- Colorectal Cancer Awareness Month

- Fire Prevention Month (The Philippines)

**"March Madness":** (United States) The NCAA Men's Division I Basketball Championship, popularly known as "March Madness" or the "Big Dance," is a single-elimination tournament to establish the champion college basketball team.

**Multi-day events:** Some March events span multiple days.

- **Nineteen Day Fast:** (Bahá'í Faith) March 2 through March 20

**Movable events:** Some events change dates from year to year.

- **Commonwealth Day:** Commwealth Day, formerly Empire Day, celebrates the establishment of the Commonwealth of Nations. It is marked by a service in

Westminster Abbey and by a speech by England's monarch to the Commonwealht nations around the world. Commonwealth Day is held annually on the second Monday in March, which can fall on any day between March 8 and March 14.

- **Canberra Day:** In the Australian Capital Territory, Canberra Day celebrates the official naming of Australia's capital city. It is also held annually on the second Monday in March, which can fall on any day between March 8 and March 14.

- **Passion Sunday:** The fifth Sunday of the Christian season of Lent is known as Passion Sunday in various Protestant denominations and by some traditionalist Catholics. Sometimes, the sixth Sunday of Lent is also known as Passion Sunday, but it is more commonly known as Palm Sunday. Passion Sunday starts the two week Passiontide, which ends on Holy Saturday, the day before Easter, commemorating the day that Jesus's body was laid in the tomb. The fifth Sunday of Lent can occur as early as March 8, and as late as April 11.

# March Zodiac Signs

From the perspective of someone on Earth, the Sun appears to move through the sky throughout the year, along a path astronomers call the ecliptic plane. The ecliptic plane is divided into twelve constellations, known as the zodiac, based on traditionally observed patterns of stars. On your birthday, you can't see your constellation, because it's part of the daytime sky.

The zodiac was first developed by Babylonian astronomers about 2,500 years ago. Because they were unaware that the Earth wobbles like a spinning top (a motion known as *precession*), they didn't make allowance for the fact that the Sun's path through the zodiac changes over time. That means there are now two sets of dates for your birth sign. The *tropical dates* are the original Babylonian dates; the *siderial dates* tell you where the Sun actually appears as it moves along its annual path.

March 11 is in Pisces in tropical dates, and is in Aquarius in siderial.

# Aquarius

**Tropical** January 20 to February 19

**Siderial** February 12 to March 14

Aquarius is one of the oldest recognized constellations, originally representing the Babylonian god Ea. In Latin, Aquarius means "water-carrier," represented in its symbol. In Greek mythology, Aquarius is sometimes associated with Deucalion, who survived a world-cleansing flood. In Chinese astronomy, it is known as the Black Tortoise of the North (北方玄武, Běi Fāng Xuán Wǔ).

In astrology, Aquarius is considered to be masculine and extroverted, and despite the name is an air sign. Aquarians are supposed to be philanthropical, inventive, and individualistic.

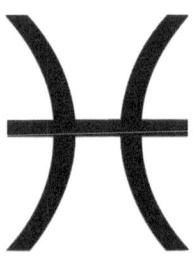

# Pisces

**Tropical** February 20 to March 20

**Siderial** March 15 to April 14

In the Roman legend of Venus and her son Cupid, they escaped the clutches of Typhon, known as the "father of all monsters," by transforming into fish and tying themselves together with rope. That's why the name Pisces is plural for fish. The constellation appears as a somewhat ragged "V" shape, representing the rope, with the "fish" located at the two rope ends.

In astrology, Pisces is a water sign, compatible with the other water signs Cancer and Scorpio, as well as with the earth signs Taurus, Virgo, and Capricorn. Pisceans are supposed to be imaginative, compassionate, unworldly, secretive, and escapist.

# What Day of the Week is March 11?

On what day of the week does March 11 fall?

Surprisingly, this isn't an easy question. Because the calendar year is 365 days long (366 in leap years), it doesn't divide evenly by the seven days of the week.

Also, the Earth goes around the Sun in about 365-1/4 days, so a calendar tends to drift over time. That's why the same date falls on different weekdays in different years.

This is made even more complicated by a change in calendars that took place in 1582. Our modern calendar has its roots in ancient Rome, in a calendar reform conducted by Julius Caesar. Caesar commissioned mathematicians to attack the problem, and came up with the idea of *leap years*, and thus standardized the calendar for centuries to come. This was called the *Julian calendar*.

Over time, however, the small errors in Caesar's calculation compounded. That's why Pope Gregory XIII commissioned the *Gregorian calendar*, used in most of the world today. Some countries converted in 1582, when the calendar was first developed; some converted later; other still haven't changed.

Gregorian and Julian aren't the only types of calendars. The Hebrew year, the Islamic year, and many other calendars are used in different parts of the world and among different people.
You can convert Gregorian dates to other calendars, including the Hebrew calendar, the Islamic calendar, and even the Mayan calendar by visiting the Fourmilab Calendar Converter at http://www.fourmilab.ch/documents/calendar/.

A 50-year brass perpetual calendar.

# Copyright, Credit, and Contact

## Follow Us

Our blog Dobson's Improbable History features short articles on events and people associated with each day, and updates several times each week. Get the latest on Twitter @SidewiseThinker.

## Sources and Art Credits

All art and photographs are either in the public domain or used under a Creative Commons license. Attribution is provided where requested by the copyright owner or when of historical significance, listed below.

- The cover photograph of the basalt statue of Tuthmosis III was released into the public domain by its author, Chip Dawes. The statue itself is in the Luxor Museum, located in Luxor, Egypt.

- The illustration of the month of March on the back cover and on page 54is from the French Gothic illuminated manuscript *Les Très Riches Heures du duc de Berry* by the Limbourg Brothers, Jean Colombe, and another painter whose name is lost to history. It is in the public domain because its copyright has expired.

- The illustration of Johnny Appleseed (Jonathan Chapman) is from the 1862 book *A History of the Pioneer and Modern Times of Ashland County* by H. P. Knapp, published by J. B. Lippincott & Co. The artist's name is unknown. It is in the public domain because its copyright has expired.

- The photograph of King Moshoeshoe I of Lesotho was taken in the 1800s. The original is in the Bensusan Museum in Johannesburg, South Africa. It is in the public domain because its copyright has expired.

- The seal of the Bureau of Indian Affairs is in the public domain as a creation of the U.S. federal government.

- The photograph of the Brooklyn Bridge during the Great Blizzard of 1888 was taken for *Life* Magazine, and is in the public domain because its copyright has expired.

- The photograph of FDR signing the Lend-Lease Act is a work for hire created prior to 1968 by a staff photographer at New York *World-Telegram & Sun*. It is part of a collection donated to the Library of Congress. Per the deed of gift, New York *World-Telegram & Sun* dedicated to the public all rights it held for the photographs in this collection upon its donation to the Library.

- The photograph of Johnny Knoxville at the 2011 San Diego Comic Con is by Gage Skidmore, and licensed under the Creative Commons Attribution-Share Alike 3.0 Unported license.

- The publicity photo from *Family Affair* is in the public domain, because publicity photos are generally printed without copyright notice and made freely available to the public.

- The 1921 publicity photo of Lillian and Dorothy Gish from *Orphans of the Storm* is from the George Grantham Bain Collection in the Library of Congress' Prints and Photographs Division. According to the Library, there are no known restrictions on the use of this photograph.

- The "Don't Panic" symbol from *The Hitchhiker's Guide to the Galaxy* is by Dan Gerhard. The copyright holder of this file allows anyone to use it for any purpose, provided that the copyright holder is properly attributed.

- The publicity photo of Lawrence Welk and Norma Zimmer is in the public domain, because publicity photos are generally printed without copyright notice and made freely available to the public.

- The official Supreme Court portrait photograph of Antonin Scalia is in the public domain as a work of the U.S. federal government.

- The 1986 photograph of Harold Wilson is by Allan Warren and is licensed under the Creative Commons Attribution Share-Alike 3.0 license.

- The 2007 photograph of Bobby Abreu was taken by "Googie Man" and is licensed under the Creative Commons Attribution Share-Alike 3.0 Unported license.

- Benjamin West's painting *The Death of General Wolfe* is in the public domain because its copyright has expired. The original hangs in the National Gallery of Canada.

- The photograph of the Oscar Mayer Wienermobile was taken by Cory Doctorow and is licensed under the Creative Commons Attribution-Share Alike 2.0 Generic license.

- The photograph of Calvin Coolidge awarding the Medal of Honor to Richard Byrd and Floyd Bennett is from the Library of Congress Prints and Photographs Division. It is in the public domain as a work of the U. S. federal government.

- The photograph of Geraldine Farrar is part of the George Grantham Bain collection at from the Library of Congress Prints and Photographs Division. It is in the public domain because its copyright has expired.

- The photograph of Lyndon Johnson meeting with civil rights leaders is in the Lyndon Baines Johnson Library and Museum. It is in the public domain because it is a work of the U.S. federal government.

- The photograph of Alexander Fleming is in the public domain because it is a work of the U.S. federal government.

- The photograph of aquamarine has been released into the public domain.

- The photograph of daffodils is by Myrabella, and is licensed under the Creative Commons Attribution-Share Alike 3.0 Unported license.

- The 1917 Women's Suffrage demonstration comes from the Library of Congress, Prints and Photographs Division, LC-USZ62-31799 DLC

- The 50-year perpetual calendar photograph is in the public domain.

www.ingramcontent.com/pod-product-compliance
Lightning Source LLC
Chambersburg PA
CBHW030521290526
45786CB00004B/1558